Examples Of Modern British Art: Forty Masterpieces By The Most Celebrated Painters Of The English School From Hogarth To The Present Day : Reproduced By The Permanent Woodbury Process : With Biographical Sketches Of The Artists

Bickers and Son

EXAMPLES OF MODERN BRITISH ART.

EXAMPLES OF
MODERN BRITISH ART.

FORTY MASTERPIECES

BY THE

MOST CELEBRATED PAINTERS OF THE ENGLISH

SCHOOL FROM HOGARTH TO THE

PRESENT DAY.

REPRODUCED BY THE PERMANENT WOODBURY PROCESS.

WITH BIOGRAPHICAL SKETCHES OF THE ARTISTS.

LONDON:

BICKERS AND SON, LEICESTER SQUARE.

1877.

CHISWICK PRESS:—C. WHITTINGHAM, TOOKS COURT,
CHANCERY LANE.

PREFACE.

N the brief space allotted to our disposal, we have endeavoured to present to our readers characteristic examples of the works of the most eminent of the British Artists who flourished from the end of the eighteenth to the middle of the nineteenth century. Many celebrated men have, for various reasons, been excluded: no room could be found for Romney, Fuseli, Stothard, Blake, Opie, and others, who deserve honourable record among the best of the English Painters. It is probable that a second series may, at some future day, do justice to the names of these old favourites.

Experience teaches us that photographic reproductions from engravings are much more satisfactory than those from oil-paintings: we have, therefore, given transcripts of the works of Bartolozzi, Woollett, Doo, Robinson, Finden, Wallis, and other celebrated engravers, which have been very faithfully rendered by the Woodbury Permanent Process. Questions of copyright and adaptability have done much to influence the choice of subjects, which we trust will be found sufficient to give a general idea of the style of each painter.

The memoirs are necessarily short. Those who desire better information concerning the lives of British Artists cannot do better than consult Redgrave's "Century of Painters of the English School"— which contains one of the most charming series of art-biographies that has ever been written.

LIST OF THE PICTURES.

LIST OF THE PICTURES.

WILLIAM HOGARTH,

HE founder of the English School of painting, was born in London on the 10th of December, 1697. He was the son of a schoolmaster, and displayed very early in life an inborn love of drawing; making sketches even on his school exercises, as no doubt many a young artist has done both before and since. Perceiving this talent, his parents wisely refrained from discouraging it, and, not having the means to give him an art education, did the best they could by apprenticing him to a silversmith and engraver, named Ellis Gamble, who lived in Cranbourne Alley.

After patiently serving an apprenticeship of seven years, Hogarth entered the drawing school, then in St. Martin's Lane. His first picture, called "The Taste of the Town," was engraved in 1724; it is full of that keen insight into character and knowledge of human life which enabled him in so many of his later works to satirize the follies of his time. Besides painting pictures, he illustrated books of various kinds, in order to gain sufficient money to assist his widowed mother and his fatherless sisters.

On the 23rd of March, 1729, Hogarth married clandestinely, and much against her father's will, Jane, the only daughter of Sir James Thornhill, the President of the St. Martin's Lane Academy and Court Painter to George I. The marriage proved a happy one, for although her father's wrath was at first great, it was overcome by the intercession of his wife and daughter, as well as by the rise of his ambitious son-in-law. Hogarth's activity and perseverance were enormous; he became a popular portrait painter, and generally had more commissions on hand than he had time in which to execute them.

Hogarth's best pictures are, as everyone knows, taken from real life, showing society in all its stages and in every grade. His famous series called the "Marriage à la Mode" in six scenes, painted in 1750, is now in the National Gallery; we must also notice "The Harlot's Progress," which appeared in 1734; "The Rake's Progress," which was engraved in the following year; and the picture we have chosen for reproduction, "The March of the Guards to Finchley," which was painted in 1750; it was sold by lottery; each purchaser of a print at seven shillings and sixpence had one ticket, and the trustees of the Foundling Hospital were fortunate enough to be the winners.

During the latter part of his career Hogarth lived during the summer in a little house at Chiswick; and in the winter months in Leicester Fields, where he died, by no means rich, on the 26th of October, 1764. He was buried in Chiswick Churchyard, where there is a monument to his memory.

RICHARD WILSON.

ICHARD WILSON, the third son of a clergyman, was born at Pinegas in Montgomeryshire, in 1713. Owing to the influence of his uncle, Sir George Wynn, who took him to London when quite young, he received a certain amount of tuition in art from a painter of little note, named Wright.

In 1748 the young artist was considered worthy to paint portraits of the Prince of Wales and the Duke of York, to be presented to their tutor, who was afterwards Bishop of Norwich. At the age of thirty-six, Wilson had managed to save sufficient money to enable him to go to Italy, and it was there that, by a happy accident, his attention was drawn to a style of art which was infinitely better suited to his talent. It is related that as he was waiting to see the Italian artist Zuccharelli, finding the time long, he amused himself by drawing the view which lay before him, through the open window; this he did with so much skill that when Zuccharelli saw the sketch, he advised Wilson to study landscape painting. In this he was very successful, as far as art was concerned, but as the taste for nature was at that time but slowly growing, he did not find it a profitable employment for a man of his limited means. His chief works are full of classical feeling; among them may be named " The Death of Niobe," " Morning," " View of Rome," " Phaeton," " Celadon and Amelia," " The Tiber, near Rome," " Adrian's Villa," " Temple of Venus at Baiæ," and " Nymphs Bathing," from which it is easy to see that he did not care to paint a scene simply for its own loveliness, but only when it was invested with historical or mythological interest.

Wilson was never a favourite with his brother artists; even Sir Joshua Reynolds was his enemy, and it is a blot on the character of that great man, that he allowed himself to speak and act ungenerously towards his rival. At the latter part of his long life, when it was almost too late to recompense him for the privations he had borne so long, Wilson became the possessor of a small estate in Wales, on which there was a lead mine. On this property, which had been left him by his brother, he lived in great retirement, working little, but wandering much around his pretty dwelling; he however never recovered his long-tried health and spirits, and eventually died a peaceful death, in May, 1782.

SIR JOSHUA REYNOLDS.

OSHUA REYNOLDS, the son of the master of a small grammar-school at Plympton in Devonshire, was born on the 16th of July, 1723. It was the original intention of his father to educate him for the medical profession, but long before the time for final decision had arrived, the young man had so fully set his mind on becoming a painter that all idea of making him a doctor was abandoned. In 1741 young Joshua was apprenticed to Thomas Hudson, a portrait painter of some eminence in London, with whom he remained two years. He then took lodgings in St. Martin's Lane, and began painting on his own account. Meeting with no great success in London, he returned to his native county; and in 1745, took a house at Plymouth and there painted the portraits of various members of several Devonshire families; among others, that of Miss Chudleigh, a lady of rare beauty, and Captain Hamilton, a scion of the noble house of Abercorn.

In 1749 Reynolds made a voyage to the Mediterranean in a ship commanded by the famous Captain Keppel, and before returning to England spent three years in Italy studying the Old Masters. After a short visit to his native county, he again set up his studio in St. Martin's Lane, and from that time his popularity increased so rapidly that, in 1755, he made engagements for painting the portraits of no less than one hundred and twenty-five persons, mostly members of the aristocracy. In 1768 he was by common consent elected the first President of the then recently established Royal Academy, and, in celebration of the event, received the honour of knighthood. Later, he succeeded Allan Ramsay as chief painter in ordinary to King George III. By that time, finding his sitters numerous and his income enormously increasing, he removed to a larger and more pretentious dwelling in Leicester Fields, now known as 47, Leicester Square. Here, with one of his sisters as a companion, he lived in luxury, esteemed and admired by all who knew him.

Sir Joshua died on February 23, 1792, and was buried with great pomp and ceremony, amid signs of almost universal sorrow, in the crypt of St. Paul's Cathedral.

THOMAS GAINSBOROUGH.

HIS celebrated artist was born in the spring of the year 1727, at Sudbury, a small town in West Suffolk, where his father was a clothier. Thomas was the youngest of three sons, and showed signs of talent at a very early age: he made a number of sketches of the scenery around his native place, and local tradition still loves to point out his favourite views. It is believed on very authentic grounds that he went to London for the education necessary to cultivate his genius when only fourteen years of age. He there studied under Hayman, a painter of some repute, and one of the original founders of the Royal Academy. He remained in London four years, during which time he very rapidly mastered the secrets of his art; and then returned to Sudbury. Here he fell in love with and married Margaret Burr, a young Scotchwoman, and the youthful pair left Sudbury for Ipswich, where they took a house at the modest rental of six pounds per annum. Soon afterwards Gainsborough made the acquaintance of Philip Thicknesse, the governor of Landguard Fort, near Harwich, who for many years was his chief patron, but being of a somewhat tyrannical nature, he became at length more of an encumbrance than an aid. In 1760 Gainsborough left Ipswich and settled at Bath, where he made a great reputation as a portrait-painter. Sir Joshua Reynolds, when delivering one of his lectures to the students of the Royal Academy on the " Character of Gainsborough," said of that artist " whether he most excelled in portraits, landscapes, or fancy pictures, it is difficult to determine."

When the Royal Academy was founded in 1768, Gainsborough was elected one of the original members. In 1774 he went to London and rented part of Schomberg House, Pall Mall. He was passionately fond of music; and was extremely kind and thoughtful in all his dealings with his friends, and wonderfully generous to his relations. His pictures are so numerous that we cannot pretend to give a complete list of even the principal, but among them we may draw attention to the following as being among his best: "The Blue Boy," "The Cottage Door," "A Cottage Girl with a dog and pitcher," "The Young Lavinia," "The Duchess of Devonshire," the "Portrait of Mrs. Siddons" in the National Gallery—which possesses several other good specimens of this master—and "The Boy at the Stile," presented to Colonel Hamilton in exchange for a violin. Gainsborough died of cancer on 2nd of August, 1788, in his sixty-second year, and was buried in Kew Churchyard.

JOHN SINGLETON COPLEY,

THE son of Irish parents who had not long previously settled in America, was born in Boston, United States, on July 3rd, 1737. At that time the neighbourhood of his native place was entirely destitute of any means of art-education, but by dint of perseverance young Copley derived from nature that instruction which the schools of the neighbourhood were unable to afford.

By the year 1760 the young artist had made such great progress that some pictures which he sent to London for exhibition attracted much notice, and excited the most favourable expectations of his future career. He continued to send specimens of his works yearly until 1767.

A few years later he set out on the usual painters' tour, going, by way of England, to Rome, and subsequently visiting the chief cities of Italy, and those places in Germany and the Low Countries where there was anything of interest in art. He returned to England in 1775, and soon decided to establish himself in London. Two years afterwards Copley exhibited a picture, called, in the phraseology of the day, "A Conversation," consisting of a group of portraits; and in 1779 was elected full member of the Royal Academy. About this time he painted his famous picture, "The Death of Lord Chatham," which was extremely popular, and is still much admired; it is now in the National Gallery. He then commenced a series of historical and political pictures, among the most admired of which are the fine works called "Charles the First ordering the Arrest of the Five Members," "The Death of Major Pierson," and "The Defeat of the Spanish Floating Batteries at Gibraltar."

Copley died on September 9th, 1815, possessed of great wealth, at his house in George Street, Hanover Square, where for many years his son, the celebrated Lord Lyndhurst, afterwards lived.

BENJAMIN WEST,

HE second President of the Royal Academy, was born on the 10th of October, 1738, at Springfield, in Pennsylvania, of parents who were descendants of an old family of English Quakers, who had long previously emigrated to America. Benjamin was born to be a painter, for he displayed unmistakable signs of artistic talent when quite a child. It is said, that when only seven years old he drew a striking and graceful likeness of his infant sister as she lay sleeping in her cot. A friend who had recognized his skill took him to Philadelphia, where he studied the rudiments of art, with much success, under an artist named Williams.

In his eighteenth year young West set up as portrait painter; and after having made sufficient money to defray the expenses, he determined to visit Europe. In 1760 he arrived in Rome—the paradise of all young artists; thence he travelled to Florence, Bologna, and other cities of Italy, to feast his eyes on the treasures of art which they so proudly possess. In the summer of 1763 he arrived in London provided with introductions, and not unheralded by a somewhat exaggerated reputation.

In 1766 West exhibited in his own house his picture of "Orestes and Pylades," now in the National Gallery. He was soon afterwards recommended to the notice of George III. by the Archbishop of York, for whom he had painted a picture called "Agrippina with the Ashes of Germanicus," and from that time he became the object of the King's almost unceasing patronage. He was one of the original foundation members of the Royal Academy, and usually contributed at least three or four works annually to the exhibitions.

On his election as President he was offered the honour of knighthood, but this he steadfastly declined on account of its being inconsistent with his religious opinions. During the latter part of his life West painted a series of paintings of religious subjects on a large scale; chief among these are, "Christ Healing the Sick," now in the National Gallery, "Christ Rejected," and "Death on the Pale Horse."

Benjamin West died at his house in Newman Street, March 11th, 1820, in his eighty-second year, and was buried with much pomp in St. Paul's Cathedral.

6

GEORGE MORLAND,

HE son of Henry R. Morland, a painter and engraver of some note, was born in the year 1763. As he was a great favourite with his father, and very early showed signs of an artistic taste, his parent apprenticed the youth, when he was fourteen years of age, to himself. Before this time, however, young Morland had exhibited sketches at the Royal Academy. In many respects his training was most unfortunate, for his father was long past middle age at the time of his son's birth, and was imbued with all an old man's querulousness and love of discipline, which, as he grew older, his son greatly resented.

Deprived of all the natural outlets of boyish nature, and compelled to devote himself entirely to his studies, it is no wonder that the youth broke loose from the bonds of such a severe restraint; much of his subsequent dissolute conduct may be regarded as only a natural result of a too rigid education.

When George Morland left his home he went to lodge at the house of William Ward, a mezzotint engraver, and for a time, actuated, probably, by a really sincere attachment to the sister of his landlord, worked steadily, painting pictures of rural domestic scenes. in July, 1786, they married, and shortly afterwards a double relationship was established between him and his friend Ward, who married one of Morland's sisters. Marriage, however, did nothing towards reforming Morland's character, and he lived in the most recklessly extravagant fashion as long as he could paint fast enough to obtain the means; eventually he was arrested for debt, and reduced to the extremity of beggary. With all this, his works were very popular and often remarkably clever. "The Gipsies," dated 1792, the time when his short spell of prosperity was at its height, was exhibited in the International Exhibition of 1862, and received much admiration. After 1802, when he was released from his obligations under the terms of a new Act, Morland's career was a rapid decline of misery, aggravated by useless self-reproach, until he died in a sponging-house in Coldbath Fields, on the 29th of October, 1804. His wife, who was always devoted to her worthless husband, died scarcely a week afterwards from a broken heart, and was interred in the same grave.

A good example of Morland's paintings, " The Reckoning," is in the South Kensington Museum.

SIR THOMAS LAWRENCE, P.R.A.,

THE most popular painter of the early part of the present century, was born at Bristol on the 4th of May, 1769.

His father, after having unsuccessfully followed various professions, was at that time an innkeeper, and a few years after the birth of his famous son, the youngest of sixteen children, removed from Bristol to Devizes, where he became landlord of the " Black Bear," a well-known posting-house. The young Thomas was from the very first a most unusually precocious child; when he was no more than seven years old he not only drew very graceful and accurate likenesses, but recited poetry, for which he had always a strong love, with really appreciative feeling. In 1779 the family again removed—this time to Oxford, where the talents of the boy attracted many patrons, and where he first painted for money.

Not long afterwards the elder Lawrence, being in poor circumstances, decided on turning the genius of his son to account, and took a house in Bath; here the young man painted portraits at the rate of a guinea and a guinea and a-half apiece, and his fame spread rapidly. Mrs. Siddons sat to him as " Zara," and Sir Henry Harpur, a local dignitary, was anxious to adopt him as his son.

In 1787 Lawrence went to London and entered the Royal Academy as a student. His rise in life was from this time very rapid. In 1791 he was elected an Associate of the Royal Academy, and upon the death of Sir Joshua Reynolds he was made " Painter to the King " in his place. In 1794 Lawrence became a full member, and on the death of West, in 1820, he received the honour of being unanimously chosen President of the Royal Academy. He had been knighted by the Prince Regent in 1815, and in 1825 he was elected a chevalier of the " Legion d'Honneur."

Lawrence never married, but owing to his fascinating manners and brilliant conversation, added to a remarkably handsome personal appearance, he was a great favourite in society, and is said to have stirred the hearts of many of his female patronesses. His popularity as a portrait painter was such that probably no artist excelled him in the number of sitters. People of all ranks and classes flocked to his studio; for he not only rendered their likenesses with truth and skill, but by his extremely graceful drawing enhanced the charms of beauty, and endowed even ordinary features with at least a pleasant air and expression. •

Sir Thomas Lawrence died, after a short illness, on the 7th January, 1830, and was buried in St. Paul's Cathedral, with remarkable signs of honour and respect.

•   3

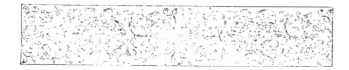

JOSEPH MALLORD WILLIAM TURNER,

HE son of a hair-dresser, was born in Maiden Lane, Covent Garden, on the 23rd of April, 1775. Owing to the friendship of Girtin, the water-colour painter, he had, as a lad, early opportunities of studying the rudiments of his art in the house of the well known art-patron, Dr. Monro. At fourteen years of age, he entered the Royal Academy Schools, and as early as 1799 was elected an Associate, and in 1802 he was made a Royal Academician. Having attained this honour, he allowed himself time for a tour in France and Switzerland, which resulted in the production of some of his finest works. In 1807 he was appointed Professor of Perspective in the Royal Academy, and about this time painted such masterpieces as "The Wreck of the Minotaur," "The Shipwreck," and "The Gale." In this year, also, he began to publish his "Liber Studiorum," a work almost unrivalled in value for art instruction. He resided successively in Harley Street, at Hammersmith, and at Twickenham, in order to be near the Thames. Five years later he removed to a house, now No. 47, in Queen Anne Street.

During his long career of prosperity, Turner remained a churlish, somewhat misanthropic man; and though he had a keen sense of humour, and was sometimes eccentrically witty, scarcely ever cared to join in any social festivities.

His most famous pictures are—"Calais Pier," exhibited in 1803 ; "Ulysses deriding Polyphemus," in 1829 ; "Childe Harold's Pilgrimage," in 1832, "The Fighting Téméraire," in 1839 ; "The Fall of Carthage," "Richmond Hill," "Heidelberg Castle," "The Parting of Hero and Leander," "The Canal at Venice," "The Golden Bough," &c.

His water-colour paintings are now eagerly sought for. As a book illustrator he was marvellously successful; and his best drawings were beautifully engraved in " Rogers' Italy," "The Rivers of France," "Southern Coast Scenery," and "England and Wales."

Turner died suddenly in lodgings at Chelsea, where he had been living under an assumed name, on December 19th, 1851, unmarried, and almost friendless; he had been in the habit of absenting himself from home during the latter part of his life, and his death occurred unknown to most of his fellow artists. He bequeathed the bulk of his property and paintings to the nation, for the benefit of art and the education of artists ; and the National Gallery now contains a fine collection of more than a hundred of his pictures.

9

JOHN CONSTABLE

WAS born at East Bergholt, a little village in Suffolk, on June 11th, 1776. His father was a miller, a man of some property and position, who intended that his son should follow the same calling; but the young artist showed such a strong preference for painting that after a year's trial he was allowed to give free scope to his taste. In 1800 he was admitted as a student of the Royal Academy, where he was assisted in his studies by R. R. Reinagle. Although he attempted portrait-painting during his early years with varying success, he, from the very first, displayed a marked and peculiar talent for landscape art. He was always firmly convinced that he had it in him to produce works of the highest class, though he fully recognized the fact that their merits might remain unnoticed by his immediate contemporaries.

In 1816 Constable married, and settled in a house in Charlotte Street, Fitzroy Square, where, with the exception of several trips into the country for the purposes of his art—to which he was faithfully devoted—he resided until 1820, when he took a cottage at Hampstead, for the sake of the lovely scenery and extensive views. He was elected a member of the Royal Academy in 1829, when he had been an associate for ten years. After several years of imperfect health, he died at his beloved Hampstead on the 1st of April, 1837.

As he had himself surmised, Constable's reputation was greater and his works were more generally admired after his death than during his life. It is strange that he met with more appreciation from the hands of French critics than from those of his native land. His most famous pictures are " The Valley Farm," a work which will ever have an enduring charm ; " The Corn Field," or " Country Lane ;" and " View on the River Stour." The Sheepshanks' Gallery possesses six other of his important works. He was one of the most truly original landscape painters we have ever had, and kept with rare fidelity to nature.

AUGUSTUS WALL CALLCOTT

WAS born at Kensington Gravel Pits, then a really country hamlet, on February 20th, 1779. He was a younger brother of the celebrated musician, Dr. Callcott, and was himself a chorister in Westminster Abbey until his voice broke, and a passion for another branch of art overcame his love of music. As a youth, he studied under Hoppner, the artist, and began life as a portrait painter. His first exhibited picture was a " Portrait of Miss Roberts," which appeared in 1799. In 1802 he discovered that his natural taste lay in another direction, and abandoned portraiture for landscape painting.

In 1810, Callcott was made a member of the Royal Academy, and for many years was a constant contributor to its exhibitions. In February, 1827, he married, and shortly afterwards started on a tour through Italy. On his return, he took a house in the " Mall," and became a fashionable artist. His wife, who was an accomplished woman, assisted him much by her literary labours on art subjects.

On the accession of Her Majesty, in 1837, Callcott, who was then one of the most favoured artists of the day, received the honour of knighthood. His works are almost all views of English scenery, though he sometimes varied them by producing figure subjects in conjunction with landscape. Some of his best known paintings are—" The Old Pier at Littlehampton," " A Calm in the Medway," " Rochester," " Entrance to the Pool of London," and " Dutch Peasants returning from Market." Callcott was a pleasant, kindly-natured man, exceedingly generous to young and struggling members of his own profession. His house was a favourite resort of men of taste in art and literature, and was brightened by the conversation of Lady Callcott, who in her latter years, though a confirmed invalid, took a never-failing interest in everything tending to aid in the advancement of culture. Callcott died in November, 1844, beloved and deeply regretted by all who had possessed the pleasure of his acquaintance.

11

THOMAS UWINS

AS born at Pentonville on the 25th of February, 1782. In his sixteenth year he was apprenticed to an engraver, with whom, however, he did not remain long, for in 1797 he was entered as a student of the Royal Academy. As early as 1808, Uwins was employed in designing illustrations for books : these were in most cases simply frontispieces, vignettes, or title-page adornments, but they displayed remarkable grace. A year later he was elected an Associate of the Society of Painters in Water-Colours, and in the following year became a full Member; he afterwards acted for a short time as secretary to that institution. In 1814 Uwins, went for the benefit of his health on a visit to the South of France; while there he made many sketches and studies, and commenced painting in oil. He returned to England about 1817 or 1818, and for the next few years lived in Edinburgh, where he was very successful as a portrait painter.

In 1824 Uwins went to Italy, and spent seven years in wandering in that country, gathering materials for a new style of painting, with which, on his return to England, he secured a lasting claim to recognition. The pictures he exhibited at the Royal Academy in 1832 earned for him the title of Associate, and, rapidly rising in public esteem, in the next year he was elected an Academician. In 1844 he was appointed Librarian to the Royal Academy; in 1845, Surveyor of her Majesty's Pictures; and in 1847, Keeper of the National Gallery. He resigned the two latter offices in 1855, and finding his health failing, went to live in quiet seclusion at Staines : here he spent the remainder of his days, and died at the age of seventy-five, in August, 1857.

His best pictures in the National Collections are " Le Chapeau de Brigand," " The Vintage in the Claret Vineyards," in the National Gallery; and " The Italian Mother teaching her Child the Tarantella," and a " Neapolitan Boy decorating the Head of his Innamorata," in the South Kensington Museum.

11

JOHN BURNET

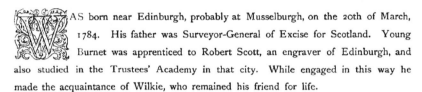 AS born near Edinburgh, probably at Musselburgh, on the 20th of March, 1784. His father was Surveyor-General of Excise for Scotland. Young Burnet was apprenticed to Robert Scott, an engraver of Edinburgh, and also studied in the Trustees' Academy in that city. While engaged in this way he made the acquaintance of Wilkie, who remained his friend for life.

In 1806, Burnet went to London and found employment as an engraver for Britton and Brayley's "England and Wales" and Cooke's "Novelists." In 1810 Wilkie entrusted him with his picture of "The Jew's Harp" for engraving; in this he was so successful that from that time his reputation was secured. Having gained money in this way he was encouraged to visit Paris, where, during some five months of the year 1815, he studied constantly in the Louvre. On his return to London he produced numerous line-engravings of a fine character, mostly renderings of Wilkie's best known works.

Besides being an engraver, Burnet was a painter and a writer upon art. His best picture is his "Greenwich Hospital and Naval Heroes," which he painted for the Duke of Wellington, and which was exhibited at the British Institution in 1837. As a writer, he will be long remembered by his many treatises on the principles and practice of different branches of art. In spite of much labour and considerable success his later years were passed in comparative poverty; until, in 1860, his name was placed upon the Civil List, and he received a pension which enabled him to live at least in comfort till he died at Stoke Newington, on the 29th of April, 1868, aged eighty-four.

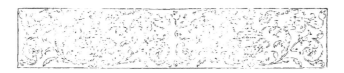

SIR DAVID WILKIE,

THE third son of his father's third wife, was born in the year 1785 at Cults, in Fifeshire. Brought up in the seclusion of a Scotch manse—for his father was minister of the parish—he had during his early years but few opportunities of cultivating his precociously developed talent. It was the wish of the whole family that David should enter the Church, but in 1799 the lad had so far gained over his father to his side, that he was sent to the Trustees' Academy in Edinburgh, where four years later he won the ten-guinea premium for the best painting of the term; the subject was "Callisto in the Baths of Diana." In 1804 he paid a short visit to his home, and during that time painted a picture called "Pitlassie Fair," the details of which were supplied by the real incidents of a neighbouring festival, and which he sold for twenty-five pounds. At this time too he painted a few portraits of friends and relatives, and having realized a little money, he started, in May, 1805, to try his fortune in London.

Wilkie's first endeavour on his arrival in the metropolis was to obtain an entrance to the schools of the Royal Academy. He soon afterwards produced "The Village Politicians," one of his best works, which was followed by "The Blind Fiddler," now in the National Gallery, and "The Rent Day," which procured for him in 1809 the title of Associate; and in 1811 he was made a full Member of the Royal Academy. In the same year he exhibited "The Village Festival," which met with universal admiration. In 1814 he went abroad, and while in Paris studied at the Louvre, and on his return enhanced his already widespread reputation by executing such favourite works as "The Penny Wedding" and "Reading the Will." Again, in 1825, he paid a long visit to the Continent, visiting Germany, Italy, and Spain. While in Spain he painted many pictures which, owing to the influence of foreign travel, showed a marked difference in his style. He returned to England in 1829, and in 1836 received the honour of knighthood.

Of a nervously sensitive temperament, Wilkie was throughout his life subject to severe attacks of illness of a prostrating nature, and it was to one of these that he succumbed while on his return from a voyage to the East. He died suddenly, just after the ship had left Malta, and was buried at sea on the same evening, June 1st, 1841.

14

WILLIAM FREDERICK WITHERINGTON

WAS born in Goswell Street, London, on the 26th of May, 1785. He received a commercial education, and very prudently continued to pursue his business for some time after his love of drawing had induced him to gain admission to the Royal Academy School. This was in his twentieth year, and it must be presumed that he made but slow progress, for it was not until 1811 that he exhibited his first picture, a "View of Tintern Abbey," at the British Institution. At this time, and for years subsequently, his works were principally composed of landscape and figure subjects in combination.

In 1830 Witherington was elected an Associate of the Royal Academy. One of his best-known works at this period, "A Hop Garden," now in the Sheepshanks Collection, was exhibited at the British Institution in 1835. In 1840 he was made a Royal Academician.

During the next few years, Witherington wandered much among the lovely scenery of Devonshire and the Welsh Lakes, where he made careful studies from nature. Almost all the pictures ascribed to him are thoroughly English; they are pleasing, natural, and carefully composed. There are two excellent paintings by him, ".The Stepping Stones" and "The Hop Garland," in the National Gallery.

Witherington died, at the age of seventy-nine, on the 10th of April, 1865.

15

WILLIAM MULREADY

\S born at Ennis, County Clare, in Ireland, on the 30th of April, 1786. His father followed the humble trade of a leather-breeches maker, and when the future artist was an infant, removed from Ennis to Dublin, and after remaining there only two or three years, came to London, where he set up his business in Compton Street, Soho. All the general education the youth received was given by three different Roman Catholic Priests in various parts of London.

In 1800 Mulready was admitted, through the influence of Banks the sculptor, to the schools of the Royal Academy, where he showed a remarkable aptitude for drawing from the life. When only eighteen he married Miss Varley, the sister of the water-colour painter, in whose school he had studied, in company with Hunt, Linnell, and many other well-known artists. The marriage was both imprudent and unhappy.

From this time, Mulready was for many years a constant exhibiter at the Royal Academy. In 1815 he was elected an Associate, and in the very next year he was made an Academician. In the latter year he exhibited "The Fight Interrupted," now in the Sheepshanks Collection.

From this time Mulready became a great favourite with the public, and his fame rapidly spread among all classes. "The Wolf and the Lamb," an excellent study of character, "The Dog with two Minds," the "Interior of an English Cottage," (which Mr. Redgrave considers a very beautiful piece of painting), "Giving a Bite," "Choosing the Wedding Gown," "Haymaking," "The Whistonian Controversy," "First Love," "The Seven Ages of Man," and "Fair Time," are a few among his many pictures which will always retain their hold upon our affections.

Mulready's later years were passed at Kensington, first in a house in "The Mall," which appears in one of his many paintings in the Sheepshanks Collection at the South Kensington Museum, and afterwards in Linden Grove, where he died somewhat suddenly, on the 7th of July, 1863. He was buried with much honour at Kensal Green, where a monument was erected to his memory by his many friends.

BENJAMIN ROBERT HAYDON,

HE son of a bookseller of Plymouth, was born on the 26th of January, 1786. He showed an early enthusiasm for art, and though apprenticed to his father's business, refused to remain in it, and against the wishes of both his parents, set out to seek the education he desired in London.

In May, 1804, young Haydon succeeded so far as to obtain admission to the Royal Academy Schools. Probably there never was a painter who possessed a more exaggerated opinion of his own powers. His whole life was a strange medley of brilliant successes and the utmost misery. His first attempt was characteristic of his nature ; when only twenty-one he painted a " Flight into Egypt" on a large scale. The next work was " Dentatus attacked and murdered by his own soldiers," the subject of which was suggested by Lord Mulgrave, for whom the picture was executed on commission.

In 1814, Haydon accompanied Wilkie to Paris, and in the same year produced " The Judgment of Solomon," which was exhibited at the British Institution, and sold for six hundred guineas. His most ambitious work, however, was " Christ's Entry into Jerusalem," painted in 1820, which he predicted would mark an epoch in the history of English painting ! It was exhibited at the Egyptian Hall, Piccadilly, and in that way brought its author nearly £3,000.

At this time Haydon established an art school at his residence in Lisson Grove, where he painted " The Raising of Lazarus " on an enormous scale ; it contains no less than twenty figures, each 9 feet high ; it was exhibited in 1823. It is now on the entrance staircase of the National Gallery.

Haydon rarely sent his pictures to the Academy, having a strange and morbid animosity against the Academicians as a body ; he generally resorted to exhibitions of his own. In 1840, he commenced a series of lectures, which were published in 1844 and 1846. His last great works were " Nero watching the Burning of Rome," and " The Banishment of Aristides," which were exhibited in 1846. They were coldly received by the public, and this so preyed on his sensitive mind that he put an end to his life in his art studio at Connaught Terrace, on the morning of the 22nd of June, 1846.

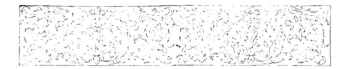

WILLIAM HILTON,

HE son of a portrait-painter who practised at Newark, was born at Lincoln on the 3rd of June, 1786. In the year 1800 young Hilton was apprenticed to John Raphael Smith, the mezzotint engraver, and six years later entered the Schools of Art at the Royal Academy.

Hilton was particularly successful as a student of anatomy and figure drawing. His early exhibited works were principally classical subjects, such as " Cephalus and Procris," "Venus carrying the wounded Achilles," and " Ulysses and Calypso ; " but in 1810 he produced a large historical picture, " The Citizens of Calais delivering their Keys to King Edward III.," which gained from the directors of the British Institution a premium of fifty guineas.

About this time he again changed his choice of subjects, and in 1811 finished a painting of the " Entombment of Christ," for which he received a second premium from the same Society of £120. For the next few years he continued this class of subjects ; in 1821 his fine picture of " Mary Anointing the Feet of Jesus " was presented by the Directors of the British Institution, by whom it had been purchased for the sum of 550 guineas, to the church of St. Michael in the City.

His next large work, " Christ crowned with Thorns," met with a similar fate : it was sold to the same purchasers, and by them presented to the church of St. Peter, Eaton Square, in 1828. The picture by which, however, Hilton is probably best known is " Edith discovering the Dead Body of Harold," which obtained a premium of 100 guineas. It is now in the National Gallery. A " Crucifixion," in the possession of the Corporation of Liverpool, is a beautiful painting in the form of a triptych.

Hilton visited Italy in 1818 in company with his friend Phillips, and in the same year reverted to his earliest style by painting " The Rape of Europa." In 1827 he was elected Keeper of the Academy, in which office he greatly endeared himself to the pupils and students. Hilton was a man of particularly retiring habits and gentle nature, and during the last few years of his life lived in seclusion. He died of heart disease, aggravated by sorrow for the death of a fond wife, on the 30th of December, 1839.

ABRAHAM COOPER

AS born in Red Lion Street, Holborn, in September of the year 1786. During his childhood he showed much talent for drawing; and as his father was an innkeeper, he was brought into frequent contact with horses, and formed a decided taste for animal subjects, which influenced the style of his numerous productions throughout his life.

His first attempt was a portrait of a favourite horse belonging to Sir Henry Meux, which was so successful that Sir Henry insisted on purchasing it, and always retained an affectionate interest in the work. After this encouragement, young Cooper set himself to master the rudiments of his art, and being unable to afford to pay for more conventional instruction, began by copying any engraving or print representing the horse or other animal which he could find, and reproducing it in colours.

At this time he was fortunate enough to attract the attention of Marshall, an animal painter of some note in his day, whose generosity in permitting the growing artist to work in his own studio was an infinite advantage to Cooper.

In 1814 his first exhibited picture appeared at the British Institution. The subject was "Tam o' Shanter;" it was purchased by the Duke of Marlborough. His next picture, representing "The Battle of Marston Moor," was sent to the Royal Academy Exhibition of 1817, and was the means of procuring his election as an Associate. Three years later he was made a full member. From that time he was a constant exhibitor at the Royal Academy during the remainder of a long life.

As might have been expected, there was but little variation in the types of his subjects and the character of their treatment. Among the more important may be mentioned, as good specimens of his style, such works as "The Pride of the Desert," the "Arab Sheik," "The Dead Trooper," "Hawking in the Olden Time," "The Battle of Bosworth Field," "The Battle of Naseby," "Richard I. and Saladin at the Battle of Ascalon," and "Bothwell's Seizure of Mary Queen of Scots." From these subjects it may be seen that his love of history—especially the more warlike portions of it, when combined with scenes in which horse-soldiers take a prominent position—had with him a predominant interest. He died at Greenwich on Christmas eve, 1868, in the eighty-second year of his age.

WILLIAM ETTY

AS born at York on the 10th of March, 1787. His father was a miller and baker. Both his parents were Methodists, and gave their son a careful religious education, beyond which his attainments in ordinary learning were of the humblest description. When only twelve years old, young Etty was apprenticed to a printer at Hull, where he remained seven years. At the end of his time, an uncle, who lived in Lombard Street, rejoiced his heart by inviting him to stay in London. Here he found the means of pursuing the studies after which he had so long hankered, and, in 1807, he became a student at the Royal Academy. He proved a most diligent pupil, and was especially successful in drawing from the nude.

After having worked at the Academy for a year, Etty became a pupil of Sir Thomas, then Mr. Lawrence. His first attempts failed to meet with favour at the hands of either the painters or the public in general, and it was not until 1811 that his first work was admitted to the exhibitions of the Royal Academy.

In 1820, he exhibited the "Coral Finders," and in the following year, "Cleopatra," both of which met with much admiration, and he then began a period of unremitting success.

Two years later Etty went to Italy, and visited Rome, Florence, Naples, and Venice. Delighted with the charms of the queen of the Adriatic, he describes it as "Venice, the birthplace and cradle of colour: the hope and idol of my professional life." He returned to London in 1824, and in the same year was elected an Associate of the Royal Academy. In 1828 he was made an Academician.

Etty's talents were of a versatile description. Among the many types he chose for his pictures, there is a wide range from such stern biblical subjects as "Judith and Holofernes," "Benaiah," and "The Eve of the Deluge," to the light and playful allegory of "Youth at the Prow, and Pleasure at the Helm." As a colourist he has been rivalled by few Englishmen, and in the portrayal of the female form and in the loveliness of his superb flesh-painting, he probably stands alone. Twelve of his best works may be seen in the National Gallery.

Etty died, beloved by all who knew him, at York, whither he had retired late in life, on the 13th of November, 1849. He was buried in the churchyard of St. Olave's, not far from the famous Minster.

WILLIAM COLLINS.

THIS charming interpreter of English rural and sea-side life was born of Irish parents in London on the 18th of September, 1787. He imbibed the first principles of art in the studio of George Morland, one of the earliest English painters who chose his subjects from the home life of the lower classes of his native land, and whose influence is very distinctly noticeable in the works of his pupil.

In 1807 young Collins entered the Royal Academy as a student, and exhibited two fine landscapes; but compelled to earn his living by painting portraits, he did not follow them up with anything at all equal to their merit until 1810, when, having saved money, he was able to choose his own subjects. He then produced a series of scenes of out-door life, such as Children bird's-nesting, or swinging on gates, Prawn-fishers, Shrimpers, Fishermen on the look out, &c., treated in a simple, life-like, and effective manner which elicited high praise from the art critics of the day.

In 1820 Collins was elected a Royal Academician, and until 1836 was a continual exhibiter of subjects similar to those by which he had made his reputation. Unfortunately for his art, he then went to Italy with a view to improving his style and enlarging his experience. After two years travelling, he returned home full of enthusiasm for the beauties of Italian scenery and Italian peasantry, and discontented with what now seemed the humdrum simplicity of every-day English life, he tried a higher style, and produced Italian landscapes, such as the "Cave of Ulysses at Sorrento," and the "Bay of Naples," following them up with the yet more ambitious subjects, "Our Saviour with the Doctors in the Temple" and the "Two Disciples at Emmaus"; these subjects were not very successful, and with true wisdom the ambitious artist returned to his first love, remaining faithful to it until his death, which took place in Devonport Street, Hyde Park Gardens, on the 17th of February, 1847.

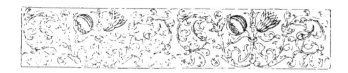

JOHN MARTIN,

ONE of the few English artists who have achieved a great position independently of the Royal Academy, was born in 1789, near Hexham, in Northumberland. He determined from the first to be an artist, but the only opening for him in his own county was in a coachmaker's office, in Newcastle, where he was apprenticed as a boy with a view to learning heraldic painting. At the end of a year, however, he quarrelled with his master and returned home. The coachmaker brought an action against the runaway, who was summoned to the town-hall to answer a charge of breach of contract. Fortunately for him, the presiding alderman, on learning the facts of the case, decided against the accuser, and with great presence of mind young Martin at once demanded the return of his indentures. The coachmaker was most unwillingly obliged to give them up, and Martin, now legally free from his hateful thraldom, became the pupil of Boniface Nunsoo, an Italian teacher of some note, and shortly afterwards accompanied him to London.

In 1806, young Martin had made so much progress as to be able to support himself by painting on glass and china, and by teaching. His first picture, "Sadak in search of the waters of Oblivion," was sold for fifty guineas, and was succeeded by "Paradise," and the "Expulsion from Paradise," all of which gave considerable promise of the grand imaginative power which subsequently characterized everything from his hand. Martin married at nineteen, and disappointed all prophecies of consequent ruin by rapidly climbing to a very high position in his profession, producing in rapid succession such extraordinary works as "Belshazzar's Feast," the "Fall of Babylon," the "Destruction of Herculaneum," the "Seventh Plague," the "Creation," &c. His twenty-four illustrations of "Paradise Lost" were scarcely less successful. He died at the Isle of Man on the 17th of February, 1854, leaving several important unfinished pictures in his studio.

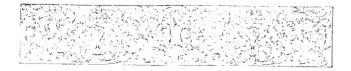

FRANCIS DANBY.

HIS historical and landscape painter, whose works greatly resemble Martin's in poetry of design and general style, was born near Wexford, on the 16th of November, 1793. Danby learnt the first principles of his art of an Irishman, named O'Connor, in Dublin, where his first picture, a landscape view, called "Evening," was exhibited in 1812. In 1813, master and pupil set off together to seek their fortunes in London, but their funds becoming exhausted before they reached the metropolis, they stopped at Bristol. Here Danby managed to sell some drawings, and with the proceeds paid O'Connor's expenses to Dublin, but he himself remained in Bristol, and for a few years supported himself by giving lessons in water-colour painting, now and then sending up an original picture to the Academy, such as the now well-known "Disappointed Love," "Clearing up of a Shower," "Sunset after a Storm at Sea," &c. His "Upas, or Poison-tree of Java," now in the South Kensington Museum, first appeared at the British Institution in 1820. In 1825, his "Delivery of the Israelites out of Egypt" having won him the honour of election as an Associate of the Royal Academy, he went to live in London, remaining there until 1829, and producing between these two dates the yet finer works, the "Opening of the Sixth Seal," and other mystical subjects from Revelations. In 1830, a quarrel with the Royal Academy drove him from England, and for the next eleven years he lived in Switzerland, giving up his time to boat-building, yachting, and the painting of unimportant pictures on commission. Two works only appeared at the annual London exhibitions during this long interim, the "Golden Age," and "Rich and Rare were the Gems she wore." In 1841, he returned to England, took up his residence at Lewisham, and began painting large subjects for exhibition at the British Institution or the Royal Academy, with all his old enthusiasm. His "Evening Gun," with the sacred pictures already alluded to, are considered his finest works. He died at Exmouth on the 7th of February, 1861.

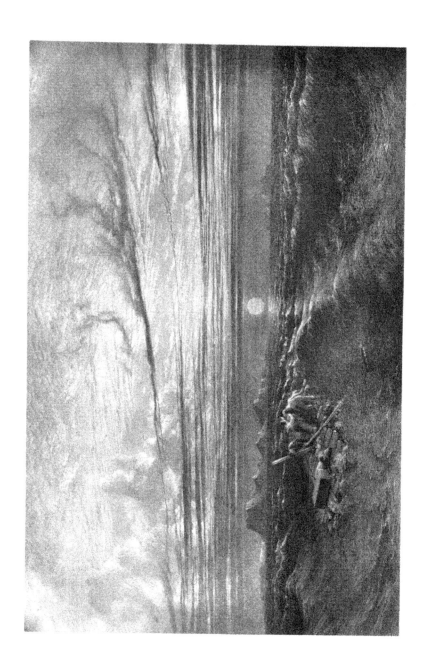

SIR CHARLES LOCK EASTLAKE.

THIS historical painter, as well known by his contributions to art-literature as by his pictures, was the son of a solicitor of Plymouth, and was born in that town on the 17th of November, 1793. Unlike most artists, who have generally had to fight their way up the ladder of success by their own unaided efforts, all was made easy for young Eastlake from the beginning. He had a good education, first at the Plympton Grammar School and then at the London Charterhouse; and when, at the age of seventeen, he expressed a wish to become a painter, he was placed under the instruction of Haydon, and entered as a student at the Royal Academy.

In 1813 he exhibited his first picture, " Christ raising the daughter of the Ruler of the Synagogue"; in 1814 he went to Paris to copy some of the masterpieces collected there by Napoleon, and on his return to England in 1815, he practised portrait painting at Plymouth for a short time with considerable success. In 1819 he started on an art tour in Italy, and pursued his studies in that country, chiefly at Rome and Ferrara; and for fourteen years sent home numerous fine works, which led to his election as an Associate of the Academy in 1827, and to the rank of Academician in 1830. At the latter date he reluctantly returned to England, and during the succeeding years devoted himself entirely to painting; producing his beautiful " Greek Fugitives," " Christ Blessing little Children," " Christ lamenting over Jerusalem," &c. Between 1841-50 he edited Kugler's " Handbooks of Paintings," &c., published his own " Materials for a History of Painting," and held the offices of Librarian of the Royal Academy and Keeper of the National Gallery. In 1857 he was elected President of the Royal Academy, and received the honour of knighthood.

From that date Sir Charles Eastlake's time was almost entirely occupied in the onerous task of selecting pictures for purchase by the British Government; and he rarely exhibited anything of his own. In the year 1865 he started on his annual tour for collecting examples of continental art for our National Gallery, was taken ill at Pisa, and died there on the 24th of December.

24

CLARKSON STANFIELD.

HIS celebrated marine painter was born at Sutherland, of Irish parents, in 1793. He began life as a sailor, but even on board ship he managed to practise drawing, sketching the vessels as they passed by, and gaining much popularity amongst the crew by painting the scenery for plays got up by them under the superintendence of their shipmate Douglas Jerrold, afterwards so well known as an author. A fall, and as it turned out, a fortunate fall, just as Clarkson was making his way in the navy, led to his discharge. On his recovery he engaged himself to the manager of the old Royalty Theatre as a scene-painter. A little later we find him in the more ambitious position of painter to Drury Lane Theatre, where he met his old friend Jerrold. In his new capacity he produced some really grand moving panoramas, which effected quite a revolution in theatrical pictorial art, and in which competent judges read the young artist's future excellence. In 1813 Stanfield became a member of the Society of British Artists, founded in that year, and in 1827 his first large picture on canvas, "Wreckers off Fort Rouge," was exhibited at the British Institution. The same year "A Calm" appeared at the Royal Academy, and from that date his progress was rapid. His naval battles, views of foreign sea-ports, mountain and river scenery, being characterized by a faithfulness to nature under all its varied aspects seldom surpassed.

In 1832 Stanfield became an Associate of the Royal Academy, and in 1835 a full Member. He died at Hampstead on the 18th May, 1867, having exhibited no less than 132 pictures in the Academy alone.

Among his most remarkable works we may name " The Battle of Trafalgar," now in the National Gallery, originally painted on commission for the United Service Club, "The Victory," with the body of Nelson on board, being towed into Gibraltar, " British Troops taking possession of the Heights and Convent of St. Bartolomeo," "The Abandoned," " Homeward Bound," " Castello d'Ischia," " Isola Bella, Lago Maggiore," and " Il Ponte Rotto, Rome."

CHARLES ROBERT LESLIE.

HIS celebrated illustrator of Shakespeare, Cervantes, Le Sage, Molière, Addison, Sterne, and other great authors, whose paintings are chiefly remarkable for dramatic power and delicate humour, was born at Clerkenwell, on the 11th October, 1794, of English parents; and when five years of age was taken by them to America. His education was begun at the Pennsylvania University, and carried on there for three years after the death of his father (which took place when he was only ten years old) at the expense of Dr. Rogers, the English professor. His mother's want of means led to his being apprenticed to Messrs. Bradford, booksellers, of Philadelphia, at the age of fourteen, in spite of his own earnest wish to become an artist. An accident, however, led to Leslie's early escape from his uncongenial employment. A portrait of Cook, the English tragedian, drawn by him, having excited the admiration of his master, Bradford, and other influential persons, a subscription was set on foot to enable him to obtain an art education in London, and he arrived there in 1811, provided with first-rate letters of introduction. He was cordially welcomed by West, Allston, and other American artists, and in 1813 was admitted a student of the Academy, gaining two silver medals soon after his entrance. From that time his progress was rapid. His first oil-paintings, the " Murder Scene from Macbeth " and " Sir Roger de Coverley going to Church," revealed his special vocation, and were rapidly followed by other similar subjects.

In 1821 Leslie was elected an Associate of the Academy, and in 1826 he became a full Member. During the succeeding years his finest works, including " The Merry Wives of Windsor," " The Taming of the Shrew," and " Uncle Toby and the Widow Wadman," were produced. In 1833 Leslie made the mistake of accepting an appointment at the American Academy at West Point, but he threw it up in the following year, returned to England, and from that time till his death in 1859 he lived and worked in London. In the years 1848 to 1851 Leslie was Professor of Painting at the Academy, and produced—in addition to his lectures in that capacity, published in 1845, under the title of " A Handbook for Young Painters "—a valuable biography of his fellow-artist, Constable.

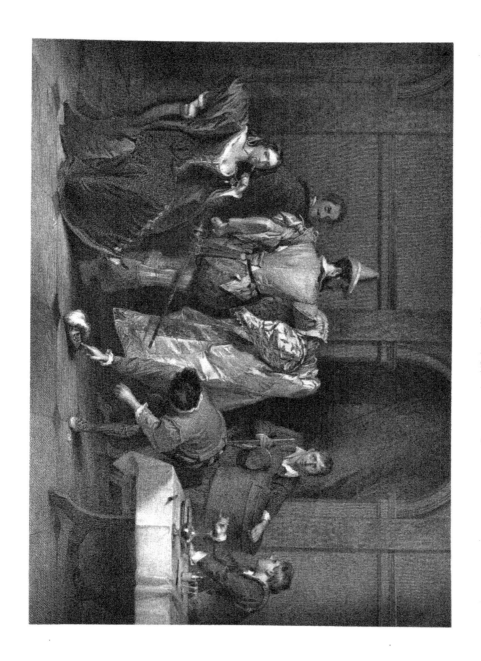

GILBERT STUART NEWTON.

HIS clever painter, one of the group of American artists who became so entirely naturalised in England as to be justly claimed as members of our modern school, was born at Halifax, Nova Scotia, on the 2nd September, 1795, and took his earliest lessons in art from his uncle Gilbert Stuart, who held a good position as portrait painter in Boston. In 1817 young Newton left America to travel on the Continent, and after visiting Italy went to Paris, where he formed a friendship with his fellow-countryman Leslie, and with him came to London by way of Belgium. At once admitted a student at the Royal Academy, he made rapid progress, exhibited a small head of great beauty, called "The Forsaken," with two other fine works, "Lovers' Quarrels" and the "Importunate Author," at the British Institution in 1821, and in 1823 began to contribute to the Royal Academy. His "Don Quixote in his Study," "Monsieur de Pourceaugnac" and "Captain Macheath upbraided by Polly and Lucy," were much admired, but were thrown into the shade by his "Vicar of Wakefield reconciling his Wife to Olivia," exhibited in 1828, which led to his election as an Associate of the Royal Academy. This was succeeded by the yet more striking "Yorick and the Grisette," "Shylock and Jessica," "Abbot Boniface," "Cordelia and the Physician," and "Portia and Bassanio."

In 1832 Newton gained the summit of his ambition in his election as a full Member of the Academy; and in the same year he paid a visit to his native land, where he married, returning to England a few months later. All now looked bright and promising, but in 1833 appeared the first symptoms of the terrible malady which darkened the remainder of his life. He began to show signs of mental aberration, exhibited but one more picture, "Abelard in his Study," and soon became totally insane. He died at Chelsea of rapid consumption on the 5th August, 1835, and was buried in Wimbledon churchyard.

DAVID ROBERTS.

THIS celebrated landscape and architectural painter, whose richly coloured interiors of Continental cathedrals are so widely known and so justly popular, was the son of a shoemaker, of Stockbridge near Edinburgh, and was born on the 2nd October, 1796. He began life as a house decorator, and practised this humble branch of the artistic profession for seven years; at the end of which probation he made a step upwards by becoming scene-painter to a company of strolling players, which led to his obtaining an engagement at Drury Lane Theatre in 1822. His first pictures on canvas were exhibited in Edinburgh and sold for very low prices; but in 1824 he joined the Society of British artists, and his views, exhibited on the walls of their gallery in Suffolk Street, brought him into general notice. In 1826 he held an engagement as scene-painter at Covent Garden Theatre, and in the same year his "Rouen Cathedral" appeared at the Royal Academy. In 1828-29 he worked with Stanfield for the "British Diorama;" and in 1830 he found himself in a position to travel, and made excursions in France and Germany, with a view to extending his range of subjects.

In 1832-33 Roberts wandered about Spain, and to this latter trip we owe some of his most valuable productions, including his large view of "Burgos Cathedral" and the well-known series of "Picturesque Sketches in Spain." On his return to England, Roberts worked at book illustrating in conjunction with Maclise for some little time, and in 1838 he made a most important art tour in Egypt and Syria, resulting in the production in 1841 of his "Ruins of Baalbec;" in 1843 of his "Gate of Cairo;" in 1845 of his "Jerusalem from the South East, the Mount of Olives;" and between 1842-49 of his well-known publication called "Roberts's Sketches in the Holy Land, Syria, and Egypt." Roberts was elected an Associate of the Royal Academy during his absence in the East in 1839, and a full Member in 1841. He died suddenly of apoplexy in London on the 25th November, 1864.

SIR EDWIN LANDSEER.

HIS great animal painter, one of the few English artists who have rivalled the realistic Dutch masters of the seventeenth century in his rendering of textures—such as fur, feathers, and horn—and whose forcible and dramatic scenes from the animal creation have done more to promote sympathy with our "dumb friends" than the efforts of any Society yet founded, was the son of John Landseer, the engraver, and was born in London on the 7th March, 1802. His talent was recognised at a very early age, and lessons in art were given to him by his father on Hampstead Heath, where he spent hours in sketching horses, donkeys, and dogs, from the life. When still a mere boy he received a prize from the Society of Arts for a drawing of a " Horse for Hunting," and he was only fourteen when he became a student at the Royal Academy and exhibited " The Heads of a Pointer Bitch and Puppy." At seventeen his " Dogs Fighting " brought him into general notice, and from that time his success was rapid and almost unprecedented.

In 1826, Edwin Landseer was elected an Associate of the Royal Academy, in 1831 he was made a Royal Academician, and in 1850 he received the honour of knighthood. His most celebrated early works were, " Alpine Mastiffs re-animating a Distressed Traveller," " The Larder Invaded," and " The Cat's-Paw ; " but their popularity was nothing to that of " Chevy Chase," "A Jack in Office," and " The Hunted Stag," produced between 1825 and 1834 ; and when they were succeeded by " The Old Shepherd's Chief Mourner "—one of the most pathetic poems on canvas ever painted,—"Tethered Rams," "The Highland Shepherd's Home," " There's Life in the Old Dog yet," the public enthusiasm knew no bounds. Admitted into the highest society, Landseer became the constant and honoured guest of the royal family, but when at the zenith of his prosperity (1851 and 1852) his life was clouded by a nervous illness which compelled him to retire into complete privacy. From this he rallied, though his powers were slightly impaired, but in 1868 a railway accident brought on a serious relapse, and he died in 1873, after three years of great suffering.

19

GEORGE LANCE.

HIS, the greatest English painter of fruit, flower, and still-life pieces, who was born at Little Easton in Essex, in March, 1802, was the son of an adjutant in the Essex yeomanry. In spite of his own early predilection for the career of an artist, he was sent to Leeds in boyhood to be trained for commerce, but he was evidently so unhappy and so unfitted for the employment chosen for him, that he was soon allowed to go to London to learn painting. He took his first lessons from Haydon, then at the zenith of his fame, and by his wish earnestly studied anatomy. He had gone through a course of study both at the British Museum and the Royal Academy before he gave proof of his special talent for the painting of still life; but his first composition of fruit and vegetables, bought by Sir George Beaumont, was of such extraordinary beauty as to decide his future career. Commissions poured in upon him, and in 1831 he produced a marvellous picture, containing a specimen of every variety of English horticulture then cultivated. He also painted historical and subject pictures with considerable spirit, giving them all a peculiar and distinctive character by the introduction of objects from inanimate nature, treated with a skill unrivalled by that of any other living artist, and almost every private and public collection in England contains one or more examples of his style. In 1836, an Interior, with monks dozing at a table covered with a copious dessert, and called " Melanchthon's first Misgiving of the Church of Rome," won for him the prize given by the Liverpool Academy for the best historical picture of the year.

We may name as among others of his best works, " The Maréchal Duc de Brion," " The Village Coquette," " From the Lake : just Shot," " Harold," " Red Cap " (in the National Gallery), and " The Lady in Waiting." Lance died on the 18th June, 1864, at his son's residence near Birkenhead, leaving behind him a daughter, who inherits his talent and seems likely ably to perpetuate his style.

THOMAS CRESWICK,

NE of the most distinguished members of the modern English school of landscape painting, whose works rival in knowledge of aerial perspective and mastery of colour those of Turner himself, was born at Sheffield in 1811, and took his first lessons in drawing in Birmingham of Mr. J. V. Barber. At the age of seventeen he went to London to seek his fortune, and his paintings being readily accepted both by the Society of British Artists and by the Royal Academy, he made the capital his home, enriching the exhibitions with scenes from Wales and Ireland. Nor did he seek subjects in his native land until 1840, when he turned his attention to the North of England, and produced some of his very finest works—the quiet beauty of our inland scenery, with its broad rivers, shady glens, and romantic dells, living again on his canvas.

In 1842 Creswick was elected an Associate of the Royal Academy, and received a premium of fifty guineas for the general excellence of his productions. In 1851 he became a full Member of the Academy, and somewhat later painted several works in conjunction with his colleagues Frith and Ansdell, who gave life and animation to his pictures by the introduction of figures and cattle. Creswick died in Linden Grove, Bayswater, after a long career of unceasing activity, and was buried in Kensal Green Cemetery.

Among his most noteworthy works we may name " England," " London Road a Hundred Years Ago," " The Weald of Kent," " The Valley Mill," " The Blithe Brook," " The Village Bridge," and " Across the Beck." The three examples of his style in our national collections, " The Pathway by the Village Church," "A Mountain Stream on the Tummel, Perthshire," and a " Summer's Afternoon," though inferior to many of his landscapes, are of considerable beauty, and may serve to give a general notion of the special character of his works.

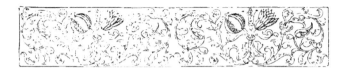

DANIEL MACLISE,

HE son of a Scotch officer, was born at Cork, on the 25th January, 1811. He was anxious to become an artist from his earliest boyhood, but his father, treating his wish as a mere whim, placed him as clerk in a banker's office in his native city. At the age of sixteen he took the law into his own hands, left his situation, and entered himself as a student in the Cork School of Art, throwing himself heart and soul into the task of mastering the first principles both of anatomy and of painting. His first commissions were portraits of officers of the 14th Dragoons, stationed for a time at Cork; and in 1826 the young aspirant for fame was able to indulge in a sketching tour in Wicklow.

In 1828 young Maclise made his way up to London, became a student at the Royal Academy, and exhibited in 1829 his first subject picture, " Malvolio affecting the Count," from " Twelfth Night." In 1831 he obtained the gold medal for the best historical composition, his " Choice of Hercules;" and in 1835 was elected an Associate of the Royal Academy, owing the honour to his well-known "Chivalric Vow of the Ladies and the Peacock," which immediately succeeded " Allhallow Eve " and the " Installation of Captain Rock," both scarcely less popular. Between 1835 and 1840 were produced some of his finest and most ambitious works—large compositions, crowded with figures and remarkable for beauty of drawing and design—of which we may name, among the most remarkable, " Macbeth and the Witches," " Olivia and Sophia fitting out Moses for the Fair," the " Banquet Scene in Macbeth," the " Ordeal by Touch," and " Robin Hood and Richard Cœur de Lion." The latter years of Maclise's life were devoted to the execution of the celebrated frescoes in the Houses of Parliament, " The Meeting of Wellington and Blucher" and the " Death of Nelson," which, unfortunately, already show signs of decay. Under the name of "Alfred Croquis" our artist produced a remarkable series of portraits of public men, which appeared in " Fraser's Magazine," and illustrated several works, including the " Pilgrims of the Rhine." He died on the 25th April, 1870.

AUGUSTUS LEOPOLD EGG,

HE son of a celebrated London gun-maker, was born in 1816. He took his first lessons in drawing of Carey, the successor of Henry Sass, in Charlotte Street, Bloomsbury, and entered the Royal Academy as a student in 1836. His first works were Italian views and illustrations of Scott's novels, but they attracted little notice. They were followed, however, by "The Victim," exhibited at Liverpool, which gave promise of great future excellence, and was so well received that its artist sent other similar subjects to the Suffolk Street Gallery. Their success encouraged him yet further, and in 1836 he began exhibiting at the Royal Academy, producing his "Spanish Girl," "Sir Piercie Shafton," "Buckingham rebuffed," at intervals of a year or two from each other. His "Lucretio and Bianca," exhibited in 1847, exalted him to high rank among contemporary artists, and in the following year he was elected an Associate of the Royal Academy. Ill-health prevented him availing himself of his improved position until 1850, when he painted "Peter the Great sees Catherine his future Empress for the first time," succeeded by "The Life and Death of Buckingham," "Past and Present," "The Night before Naseby," and "Catherine and Petruchio,"—all manifesting great imagination and artistic skill combined with a melancholy peculiarly their own.

In 1860 Egg became a full Member of the Royal Academy; but his health was declining rapidly and he was obliged to go to Algiers as a last chance of saving his life. A temporary rally ensued, but he caught cold while out riding, and died of asthma early in March, 1863. He was buried on a lonely hill near Algiers, away from his family and friends. The only work by him in our national collection is a scene from "Le Diable Boiteux," exhibited at the Royal Academy in 1844; a remarkably clever picture, but scarcely a fair example of his style, wanting as it is in the pathos so characteristic of almost everything he produced.

DOUGLAS COWPER.

UT little is known of the life of this able painter, whose early death at the age of twenty-two excited universal regret. He was born at Gibraltar on the 30th May, 1817, the son of a merchant carrying on business in that town. The early evidences of his artistic power were disregarded, and every attempt he made to obtain instruction in art was vigorously thwarted. He persevered, however, gaining a little knowledge here and a little there, until he attained his seventeenth year, and then feeling unable any longer to endure the restrictions to which he was subjected, he won a reluctant consent to his leaving home, made his way to London, obtained admission to the Royal Academy Schools, and soon carried off the silver medal for the best copy in painting of the subject for the year.

His first exhibited works, produced when only twenty years of age, were a Portrait and "The Last Interview;" followed in 1838 by "Shylock, Antonio and Bassanio;" and in 1839 by "A Capuchin Friar" and "Othello relating his Adventures,"—the latter considered his finest composition. Unfortunately the great promise given in it was destined never to be fulfilled; he exhibited no more at the Academy, his Lucy Ashton," "Proposed Elopement," "Last Farewell" and "Kate Kearney," which appeared in the Suffolk Street Gallery, and a subject from the "Taming of the Shrew," for a short time in the rooms of the British Institution, were the only other pictures he painted. The first symptoms of consumption manifested themselves only too unmistakably; he hastened to Guernsey, where his family then lived, but the fell disease which has claimed so many youthful victims was not to be eluded, and he died on the 28th November, 1839, having lived only just long enough to justify his own determination to be an artist and to show the world what great things he might have done.

WILLIAM LINTON.

HIS celebrated classic landscape painter—whose recent death, on the 18th August, 1876, has excited universal regret—was born in Liverpool in 1791, and began life as a clerk in a merchant's office in that city. Finding it impossible to reconcile himself to his duties, and believing that he had it in him to succeed as a painter, he threw up his situation about the year 1820, made his way to London, and devoted himself to the study of art. In 1821 he exhibited his first picture, "The Morning after a Storm," at the British Institution, and about the same time joined the then newly founded "Society of British Artists." The greater number of his earlier works were exhibited in their Gallery, and won for him eager recognition from the art critics of the day. Encouraged by this success he made a long art tour on the Continent, with a view to extending his range of subjects, returning to England in 1829, and producing a fine series of landscapes treated in the classic style, including the well-known "Italy," &c. He then made a second and more extended tour, visiting Greece, Sicily and Calabria, and on his return home he worked up his studies, which he exhibited in 1842, at the Gallery of the Society of Painters in Water Colours, into some fine pictures, such as the "Embarkation of the Greeks for Troy," and "The Temple of Pæstum," both of which were exhibited in Westminster Hall. In 1842 his "Lake of Orta" and "Bellinzona" appeared at the Royal Academy, and from that date he was a frequent contributor to the annual exhibitions of that Institution. During the latter years of his life he devoted some time to art literature, publishing "Sketches in Italy," in two folio volumes, in 1832, a pamphlet on "Ancient and Modern Colours," in 1852, and a book on the "Scenery of Greece and its Islands," with fine illustrations from his own hand, in 1856. Among his best works we may name "Marius at Carthage," "Jerusalem at the Time of the Crucifixion," "The Triumph of Fortuna Muliebris," and his "City of Ancient Greece."

35

CHARLES LANDSEER,

 SON of John Landseer, an eminent engraver, was born in 1799. He was the elder brother of the famous Sir Edwin Landseer, and together with him, received his early instruction in art from their father. Later in life he studied under Haydon, and in 1816 became a student of the Royal Academy Schools. While still a youth he accompanied the late Lord Stuart de Rothesay to Portugal and Rio de Janeiro. During this tour he made many drawings and sketches, which served as studies for pictures which he afterwards executed.

His first exhibited picture, "Dorothea," appeared at the Academy in 1828; in the same year he produced various scenes of Continental subjects, mostly figure subjects. In 1832 he for the second time exhibited on the walls of the Academy; the subject of his painting was "Clarissa Harlowe in the Prison Room of the Sheriff's Office;" it is now in the Vernon Collection at the National Gallery. "The Sack of Basing House," now in the National Gallery, and "The Battle of Langside," procured Charles Landseer's election as Associate of the Royal Academy in 1837.

In 1845 he was honoured with the title of Royal Academician, and in 1850 was appointed successor to the late George Jones in the Keepership of the Academy. In May, 1873, the council voted him a pension as an acknowledgment of his long and valued services.

Three of his works have been presented to the nation by the late Mr. Jacob Bell, and are called respectively, "Bloodhound Bitch and Pups," "The Pillaging of a Jew's House in the reign of Richard I.," and "The Sack of Basing House," before-mentioned. Several of Mr. Charles Landseer's works have won prizes from the Art Union Society.

THOMAS WEBSTER.

HIS well-known subject painter, whose works appeal powerfully to the sympathies of every class, and who ranks high, not only among British, but European artists, was born in Ranelagh Street, Pimlico, on the 20th March, 1800; and was taken when still a mere baby to Windsor, where his father held an appointment in the royal household. On the death of George III., the Webster family removed to London, and young Thomas was placed in the choir of the Chapel Royal, St. James's, sharing in the education given to his fellow choristers. He showed no special aptitude for music, however, and at his own earnest request was allowed to give up its study for that of painting. He entered the Royal Academy School of Art in 1820, at an age when most men have already begun fighting their own way in the world; but he made such rapid progress as to win the first medal for proficiency in painting in 1825. His " Rebels Shooting a Prisoner," exhibited at the Gallery of British Artists in Suffolk Street, in the same year, brought him into general notice, and may be said to have founded his reputation. In 1827 a portrait group of children was exhibited at the Royal Academy, followed at pretty regular intervals by such works as " The Gunpowder Plot," " The Sick Child," " The Love Letter," " The Smugglers," and " The Village School." From 1834 to 1842 Mr. Webster gave himself up almost entirely to the study of the ways and feelings of children, producing many a charming group, full of humour and character, such as " The Boy with Many Friends," " The Smile," " The Frown," " Punch," &c. In 1840 he was elected an Associate of the Royal Academy, and in 1846 a full Member. Between those dates he exhibited his celebrated " Sickness and Health," remarkable for its pathetic sadness; the " Contrary Winds," " The Dame's School," and other scenes from child-life. Every annual exhibition of late years has contained numerous examples of his style; his pictures command the highest prices, and seem likely long to maintain their popularity.

In 1876, Mr. Webster sent in his resignation, and he is now on the retired list of Royal Academicians.

THOMAS SIDNEY COOPER.

HE life of this successful exponent of the peaceful scenery of the South and the rugged beauty of the North of Britain has been one long struggle with difficulties beneath which any but the most undaunted spirit must have succumbed. Born at Canterbury in 1803, he was deserted by his father when a mere child, and set to work to earn his own fortune, when, under happier circumstances, he would have been still at school Before he was sixteen he was supporting himself by selling sketches of Canterbury Cathedral, and that without having had a single lesson in drawing. In 1819 he was fortunate enough to attract the notice of Doyle the actor, who gave him lessons in perspective. Of these he availed himself with such hearty good will that his pictures soon fetched higher prices, and he was able to join the classes of Mr. John Martin, then the first teacher of drawing in North Kent. In 1824 we find Cooper realizing money at the rate of £200 a year by giving drawing lessons in Canterbury, but in 1827 his connection was ruined by the arrival of a French artist, who drew off his pupils. Nothing daunted, he joined a schoolfellow named Burgess, and went with him to seek his fortunes abroad. Landing in Calais, almost destitute, he paid his way by taking the portraits of the innkeeper and his family, and four days later left that city for Gravelines with fifty-two francs profit beyond expenses. Similar good fortune attended him wherever he went, and he soon found himself in a position to marry the lady of his choice—a resident in Brussels. Shortly after his marriage he made a tour through Holland to study the Dutch animal painters, but he was recalled to Belgium by the revolution of 1830, which compelled him to return to England, where he earned a scanty subsistence for himself and his family by making pencil sketches and drawings on wood. Gradually, however, he rose into note, exhibiting his first picture at the Suffolk Street Gallery in 1833, and becoming an Associate of the Royal Academy in 1845. From that time to the present he has been a steady contributor to our annual exhibition ; he is now a Royal Academician, and his name is known and honoured as that of a high-class landscape and animal painter throughout the length and breadth of Europe.

RICHARD REDGRAVE.

HIS popular artist, whose best works, such as "The Reduced Gentleman's Daughter," "The Poor Teacher," "The Sempstress," aim, as he himself tells us, "at calling attention to the trials and struggles of the poor and oppressed," was born at Pimlico in April, 1804. The son of a London manufacturer, his first years of early manhood were passed in his father's counting-house, where he made designs and working-drawings for the men, occasionally varying the monotony of his employment by a trip into the country to look after the interests of his firm. His father's business began to fall off when young Redgrave was about nineteen, and with a view to getting his living as an artist he began studying from the Elgin Marbles at the British Museum. In 1825 a landscape by him was exhibited at the Royal Academy, and in the following year he was admitted as a student at that institution. Determined to support himself entirely by teaching, during his own course of instruction, he took numerous pupils; and although this involved working some fourteen hours a day, and his health more than once nearly gave way beneath the strain, he managed gradually to win his way upwards. Before 1831 we find his pictures hung on the line at the Academy, and his position so much improved that he was able to give up nearly all his time to his own improvement in art. In 1831 appeared his ambitious historical picture, " The Commencement of the Massacre of the Innocents," and in 1833 his " Cymbeline" and two landscapes, none of which, however, attracted any special notice. His first great success was "Gulliver on the Farmer's Table," exhibited at the British Institution, and bought almost as soon as it was hung. From that date every Exhibition has contained one or more of his works.

Mr. Redgrave was elected an Associate of the Royal Academy in 1840, a Royal Academician in 1850, and was appointed head master of the Government School of Design in 1851. He has held numerous similar offices in succeeding years, and is Surveyor of Her Majesty's pictures, and one of the chief dispensers of art patronage of the day.

39

FREDERICK RICHARD LEE.

THIS celebrated landscape painter, whose views of Scotch and English scenery are remarkable alike for originality and faithfulness to nature, was born at Barnstaple in 1799 and began life as a soldier. After an arduous campaign in the Netherlands he returned to England invalided, and in 1818 became a student at the Royal Academy. His earliest works were exhibited at the British Institution, but in 1824 he began to contribute to the Royal Academy, and continued to do so at pretty regular intervals for the next ten years. In 1839 his "Cover Side,"—a scene in a wood, with a group of dogs, figures, and game sketched in by Sir Edwin Landseer, now in the National Gallery—was exhibited at the British Institution; and between that date and 1856 he produced a fine series of similar works, including the beautiful "Evening in the Meadows" and "A River Scene," both with cattle by Thomas Sidney Cooper, both of which are in our national collection. The succeeding years witnessed a change; for, leaving the peaceful inland scenery from which he had hitherto chosen his subjects, Lee sought his inspiration on the coast, and exhibited the "Breakwater at Plymouth," succeeded by "The Bay of Biscay" and "Gibraltar,"—all giving promise of great excellence in this new field. Lee was elected an Associate of the Royal Academy in 1834, and a full Academician in 1838. Several of his earlier works are in the Sheepshanks Collection at South Kensington, and "Near Redleaf," a study of autumnal foliage, "Gathering Seaweed," and a "Distant View of Windsor," distinctively English as they are, may be recommended to the special notice of young students of British landscape art. Some groups of fish, dead game, &c., painted for Mr. Wells, give proof that our artist could also have attained to high excellence in the delineation of still life,—a branch of art seldom successfully practised by Englishmen.

CPSIA information can be obtained at www.ICGtesting.com
Printed in the USA
BVOW09s1157130215

387651BV00011B/145/P